THE LIFE & TIMES OF
JACK THE RIPPER

D0487850

THE LIFE & TIMES OF

Jack the Ripper

BY
Philip Sugden

This is a Siena book
Siena is an imprint of Parragon Book Service Ltd

This edition first published by
Parragon Book Service Ltd in 1996

Parragon Book Service Ltd
Unit 13–17 Avonbridge Trading Estate
Atlantic Road, Avonmouth
Bristol BS11 9QD

Produced by Magpie Books Ltd, London

ISBN 0 75251 541 1

A copy of the British Library Cataloguing in Publication
Data is available from the British Library.

Typeset by Whitelaw & Palmer Ltd, Glasgow

JACK THE RIPPER

Jack the Ripper is the most notorious murderer of modern times, his name a worldwide symbol of terror. His crimes were macabre. And, of course, unsolved. But the victims were comparatively few and the geographical extent of the killing field extremely limited.

Senior detectives on the case never agreed on the true total of the Ripper's victims. Estimates ranged from four to nine. Most modern experts agree that he claimed at least four victims – Mary Nichols, Annie Chapman, Catharine Eddowes and Mary Kelly. There are strong grounds, however, for adding two more, Martha Tabram and Elizabeth Stride, making a probable tally of five or six, all prostitutes, all slain in the late summer and autumn of 1888.

Although these crimes are sometimes referred to as the 'Whitechapel murders' only two of the six were actually committed in Whitechapel. Two were perpetrated in Spitalfields, one in St George's-in-the-East and one in the City. Nevertheless, all of the murder sites are within a single square mile in the East End of London.

The Victorian East End was an area of low incomes, unemployment, homelessness and destitution. Such conditions inevitably spawned crime and prostitution. Streets like Dorset Street, Flower and Dean Street and Thrawl Street, at the heart of the murder district, were among the worst in the metropolis. Charles Booth, in his *Descriptive Map of London Poverty 1889*, marked them in black, denoting that they were 'vicious, semi-criminal'.

The Ripper's victims were mostly poor, middle-aged women, deprived of male support by broken marriages or bereavement. For such women life was especially hard. Some jobs were seasonal. And work like charring, washing and hawking was greatly oversubscribed and therefore insecure and poorly paid. Not surprisingly, prostitution became an instrument of survival. A police report of 1888 estimated the number of prostitutes working on the streets of the Metropolitan Police's H or Whitechapel Division at 1200. For a man with murder and mutilation in mind, a man like Jack the Ripper, they were the most vulnerable of targets. James Monro, Chief Commissioner of the Metropolitan Police in 1889, understood their plight perfectly: 'Scores of these unfortunate women may be seen any night muddled with drink in the streets and alleys, perfectly reckless as to their safety, and only anxious to meet with anyone who will keep them in plying their miserable trade.'

By moving from one locale to another some modern serial killers have remained at large for years and have claimed far more victims than the Ripper. But few killers have inspired the degree of fear generated by the Ripper murders and this was partly because they were so concentrated in time and place. At the height of the scare in the autumn of 1888 the inhabitants of the East End, and indeed of other parts of London, then the capital of the greatest empire in the world, lived in terror of the lone assassin.

It was a time that lingered for many years in the memories of those unfortunate enough to have experienced it. 'No one who was living in London that autumn will forget the terror created by these murders,' wrote ex-CID chief Melville Macnaghten 25 years later. 'Even now I can recall the foggy evenings, and hear again the raucous cries of the newspaper boys: "Another horrible murder, murder, mutilation, Whitechapel." Such was the burden of their ghastly song; and, when the double murder of 30 September took place . . . no servant-maid deemed her life safe

5

if she ventured out to post a letter after ten o'clock at night.'

THE FIRST MURDERS

The first murder commonly attributed to Jack the Ripper occurred in the early hours of Tuesday 7 August 1888. The place was George Yard Buildings, a tenement block in George Yard (present Gunthorpe Street), off Whitechapel High Street.

At about 4.45 that morning a waterside labourer named John Reeves left his room in the block to go to work. He descended the stairs. And there, on the first floor landing,

George Yard

he discovered the body of a woman. Middle-aged, plump and about five feet three inches in height, she lay on her back in a large pool of blood. She was fully clothed but her dark-green skirt and brown petticoat had been thrown up to expose her legs and lower torso. Horrified, Reeves stumbled down into the street and summoned a policeman.

Subsequent inquiries by the police identified the dead woman as Martha Tabram. Martha was 39. The daughter of Charles White, a Southwark warehouseman, she had married Henry Tabram, a foreman packer, on Christmas Day 1869. There were two children. But in 1875 the marriage had broken up because of Martha's heavy drinking and at the time of her death she was living at a common lodging house in George

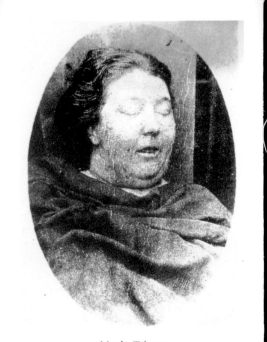

Martha Tabram

Street, Spitalfields, and supporting herself by hawking and prostitution. She was last seen alive at 11.45 on the Monday night, taking a client, a soldier, into George Yard.

Martha had died in a frenzied attack. Thirty-nine stab wounds were found on her body. Dr Killeen, who performed the autopsy, concluded that she had been killed at about 2.30 and that two different weapons had been used. Most of the wounds could have been inflicted with a penknife. But there was a deep wound in the breast that could only have been made with a strong, long-bladed weapon. This, he suggested, might have been a dagger or a bayonet. Suspicion inevitably fell upon Martha's soldier companion. However, since he had been observed with her nearly three hours before the estimated time of death, there is little reason to suppose that he was the murderer. Neither the soldier nor the real killer were identified.

Accustomed though they were to brawls and street violence, the people of the East End were shocked by the savagery of the Tabram slaying. Residents in and about George Yard immediately formed themselves into a committee, the St Jude's Vigilance Committee, to watch the streets at night. But few seem to have regarded the murder as anything more than a freak, isolated tragedy. Until, three weeks later, when another woman was killed.

At about 3.40 on the morning of Friday 31 August, Charles Cross, a carman walking to work, found the second victim lying dead in Buck's Row (now Durward Street), Whitechapel. Dominated on the north side by high warehouses, the street was narrow, dark and secluded, a favourite resort of local prostitutes. Medical opinion later placed the time of death only minutes before Cross arrived on the scene. Indeed it is more than likely that he disturbed and scared away the killer. But he neither saw nor heard anything suspicious.

The victim was soon identified as Mary Nichols, known to her friends as Polly. She had been murdered only five days after her forty-third birthday. Polly had married a printer's machinist named William Nichols when she was eighteen but had been living apart from her husband for about eight years. Since the separation her life had been spent in workhouses and common lodging houses. Like Martha Tabram she had become a heavy drinker. And like her she regularly solicited

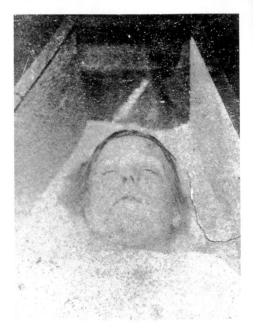

Polly Nichols

on the streets. At about 1.20 on the morning
of her death she had been turned out of a
common lodging house at 18 Thrawl Street
because she did not have fourpence, the price
of a bed. 'I'll soon get my doss money,' she
told the deputy as she left. 'See what a jolly
bonnet I've got now!' Polly must have set
about raising the money by prostitution. But
when her friend Ellen Holland met her at the
corner of Whitechapel Road and Osborn
Street about an hour later she was very drunk.
'I have had my lodging money three times
today,' she boasted, 'and I have spent it.' Mrs
Holland watched her reel away along
Whitechapel Road. Scarcely more than an
hour after that she was dead.

Polly's wounds were horrendous. Her throat
had been cut right down to the spinal
column. The murderer had then thrown up

her skirts and ripped open her abdomen, exposing the intestines. Dr Llewellyn, who conducted the post-mortem examination, believed that the murderer had inflicted the wounds with a strong-bladed knife and that he had displayed 'rough anatomical knowledge'. Beyond that there was no clues to the killer's identity.

For the first time the police began to suspect that they were dealing with a serial killer. They responded by appointing Chief Inspector Donald Swanson to oversee the investigation from Scotland Yard and by despatching one of their finest detectives, Inspector Frederick G. Abberline, into the East End to co-ordinate inquiries on the ground.

On the morning of Saturday, 8 September, a third victim fell to the knife.

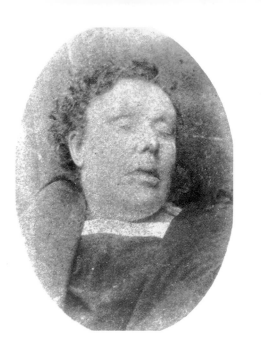

Annie Chapman

Her name was Annie Chapman. Annie was a Londoner, born about 1841 to George Smith, a private in the second battalion of lifeguards, and his wife Ruth. In 1869 she married a coachman named John Chapman but his death in 1886 left her to fend for herself. Apparently she managed to make a precarious living from crochet work, selling flowers and casual prostitution.

Annie's last home was Crossingham's lodging house at 35 Dorset Street, Spitalfields. At about 1.50 on the fatal morning Timothy Donovan, the deputy there, expelled her because she did not have enough money to pay for a bed. About four hours later her mutilated body was found only a few hundred yards away, in the dirty backyard of 29 Hanbury Street. Her throat had been ferociously severed from left to right. The

Hanbury Street

abdomen had been laid open and the murderer had lifted the intestines out of the body and deposited them on the ground above the right shoulder. The womb, together with parts of the vagina and bladder, had been removed and taken away. Dr Phillips, a police surgeon who examined the body in the backyard, noted that the contents of the dead woman's pocket – a piece of coarse muslin and two combs – had been carefully placed by her feet. 'They had apparently been placed there in order,' he said, 'that is to say, *arranged* there.'

Extensive police inquiries in the area again failed to detect the killer. But this time a witness came forward. At about 5.30 on the 8th, shortly before Annie must have been killed, Mrs Elizabeth Long saw her talking to a man of 'shabby genteel' appearance outside

No. 29. She heard the man ask: 'Will you?' And Annie answer: 'Yes.' Unfortunately Mrs Long only saw the man from behind. But she remembered that he stood only a little taller than Annie, that he looked like a foreigner and that he wore a dark coat and brown deerstalker hat. She thought he was more than 40 years old.

It was generally believed that all three murders had been committed by the same man. But there was little agreement on motive. Police inquiries failed to find any explanation of the crimes in the life histories of the victims. And their poverty, and the extent of their injuries, ruled robbery out of the question.

Dr Phillips started a new line of inquiry. Examining Annie Chapman's body, he

concluded that the womb had been extracted
by a man of anatomical knowledge and surgical
skill. It led him to speculate that the intention
of the murderer had been to secure a specimen
of this particular organ. On the face of it this
was a bizarre and unlikely theory. But then, on
the last day of the Chapman inquest, Mr
Wynne Baxter, the coroner, revealed new
evidence that reinforced it.

He related a story told to him by the sub-
curator of the pathological museum attached
to 'one of our great medical schools'.
Apparently an American had visited him
some months previously and had offered to
buy specimens of the womb for £20 each. He
wanted them, he said, to send out with copies
of a medical book on which he was engaged.
Is it not possible, asked Baxter, that some
'abandoned wretch' had learned there was

money to be made in supplying specimens of the required organ and had embarked upon murder in order to procure them?

The story sparked off a heated debate in the press. Doctors quickly pointed out that specimens for legitimate research were readily available without recourse to crime. And most of the medical schools approached by the press denied any knowledge of the American's strange request. However, two schools – those attached to University College and Middlesex Hospitals – refused to repudiate the story and, according to the press, talked mysteriously about the 'interests of justice' being imperilled by a full public disclosure of the facts.

In the midst of this furore the murderer struck again. This time two victims were slain in a single night.

DOUBLE EVENT

Between Nos. 40 and 42 on the west side of Berner Street, off Commercial Road, was a gloomy passage leading from Berner Street into a small court known as Dutfield's Yard. The entrance to the passage in Berner Street was guarded by two big wooden gates.

When Louis Diemschutz, steward of the International Working Men's Club at No. 40, drove his pony and cart up to the gates at one o'clock on the morning of Sunday, 30

Berner Street, showing entry (marked by cartwheel) to Dutfield's Yard

September, he found them wide open. This was not unusual. But as Diemschutz urged his pony through the gates and into the passage beyond it shied to the left. On the ground, on the right-hand side of the passage, lay the dead body of a woman. Her throat had been cut and a stream of blood was still trickling up the yard from the wound. There were no other mutilations.

Once again the killer had narrowly escaped discovery. When Dr Blackwell examined the dead woman at 1.16 he found parts of the body quite warm and concluded that she could not have been dead 'more than twenty minutes, at the most half an hour'. This suggests that the woman had been murdered only minutes before Diemschutz drove into the gateway.

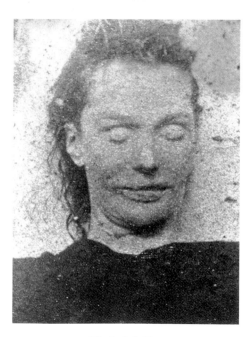

Elizabeth Stride

Only 45 minutes after Diemschutz found the body in Dutfield's Yard another grisly discovery was made in Mitre Square, three-quarters of a mile away. This was within the eastern boundary of the City of London and it was a City policeman – PC Edward Watkins – who made the discovery. When Watkins patrolled Mitre Square at about 1.30 it was deserted. But 15 minutes later, entering the square again, his lantern revealed the gruesome sight of a mutilated corpse in the darkest and southernmost corner. 'I saw the body of a woman lying there on her back,' he would tell the inquest, 'her feet facing the square, her clothes up above her waist. I saw her throat was cut and her bowels protruding. The stomach was ripped up.'

While City detectives were converging on Mitre Square the only tangible clue ever left

Mitre Square

by the murderer was discovered. At 2.55 PC
Alfred Long, a Metropolitan Police constable
on duty in Goulston Street, Whitechapel,
found a piece of the Mitre Square victim's
apron, still wet with blood, lying in the entry
to Nos. 108–119 Wentworth Model
Dwellings. Written in white chalk on the
right-hand side of the doorway, just above the
apron, was a message. It read:

> The Juwes are
> The men That
> Will not
> be Blamed
> for nothing.

This enigmatic writing is difficult to interpret.
On the face of it it suggests that the murderer
was a vengeful Jew. But the police view at the
time was that it was a deliberate red herring,

designed to throw the police off the track of the real killer by incriminating the Jews. Whatever its significance, it caused an immediate dispute between the City and Metropolitan forces. City detective Daniel Halse strenuously urged that the message be preserved until it could be photographed. But Sir Charles Warren, Chief Commissioner of the Metropolitan Police, was convinced that if it became public knowledge it would provoke anti-Jewish riots in the East End and he ordered it to be wiped away before daybreak.

In the weeks following the double murder police toiled doggedly to identify the victims and unravel the mysteries of their final hours.

The Berner Street victim proved to be Elizabeth Stride (née Gustafsdotter), a Swede

The discovery in Mitre Square

born near Gothenburg in 1843. Emigrating to London in 1866, she married a carpenter named John Stride and settled in Poplar. John opened a coffee room there but, for unknown reasons, the marriage was soon in difficulties. The couple separated. John died in Bromley in 1884. Elizabeth took to charring and prostitution, becoming a familiar figure in the streets and pubs of Spitalfields and an occasional resident at a common lodging house at 32 Flower and Dean Street. During her last few years she lived on and off with Michael Kidney, a waterside labourer. The relationship was tempestuous and there were frequent quarrels and separations. It was for this reason that on 29 September 1888, the eve of her death, Elizabeth was back at No. 32.

Elizabeth left the lodging house at about

seven that evening. She didn't say where she was going but that night she was seen several times in Berner Street.

At about 12.30, only half an hour before her body was found in the entry to Dutfield's Yard, PC William Smith saw her talking to a man in the street close by. This man was 'respectable' in appearance. He looked about 28, stood five feet seven or eight inches tall, and had a small dark moustache. He wore a dark deerstalker hat and a black diagonal cutaway coat and he was carrying a parcel wrapped up in newspaper. Even more remarkable was the story of Israel Schwartz, a passerby, who saw Elizabeth being pulled about and thrown down on the pavement outside Dutfield's Yard by a man at about 12.45. Scared, Schwartz hurried away. But he gave a good description of the man: 'age about 30,

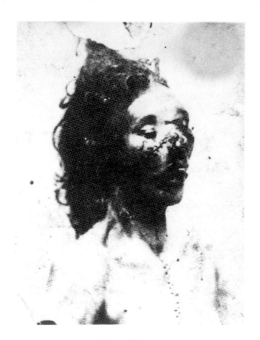

Kate Eddowes

height 5 ft. 5 in., complexion fair, hair dark, small brown moustache, full face, broad shouldered; dress, dark jacket and trousers, black cap with peak.' Within 15 minutes of Schwartz's sighting Elizabeth was dead.

The Mitre Square victim was Kate Eddowes, the chirpy 46-year-old daughter of a Wolverhampton tinplate worker. Her history was similar to that of the other victims. For many years she lived with an army pensioner named Thomas Conway but they separated about 1880, apparently on account of Kate's excessive drinking. In 1881 she met John Kelly, a labourer, and from then until her death the two were regular lodgers at 55 Flower and Dean Street. John got what work he could in the markets. Kate tried her hand as a charwoman. And in the summers they tramped the countryside together, picking hops and fruit or haymaking. There is little doubt that Kate was also a prostitute.

Incredibly Kate was in the custody of the City Police less than an hour before she was murdered. On the evening of 29 September she was found helplessly drunk in Aldgate High Street, arrested and taken to Bishopsgate Street Police Station. Placed in a cell, she slept there for several hours. Then, at one in the morning, she was discharged. 'I shall get a damned fine hiding when I get home,' she told the officer on duty.

At about 1.35 three Jews leaving the Imperial Club in Duke Street saw a man and a woman talking at the entrance of Church Passage, which led from Duke Street into Mitre Square. One of the three, a commercial traveller named Joseph Lawende, said later that the man was about thirty, perhaps five feet seven or eight inches in height and of medium build. His moustache was fair. He dressed rather shabbily. Lawende remembered a pepper-and-salt coloured jacket, a reddish neckerchief and a grey cloth cap with a peak. He had, thought Lawende, the appearance of a sailor. He did not see the woman's face but it seems likely that he had chanced upon Kate talking to her murderer. Ten minutes later her dead body was found in Mitre Square.

The throats of both victims had been severed from left to right. Elizabeth Stride suffered no further injuries. But Kate Eddowes had been horrendously mutilated after death. There were severe abdominal injuries. The head and face were slashed. And the left kidney and part of the womb had been cut out and taken away.

Some contend that Stride and Eddowes were slain by different men. However, the explanation for the disparity in the injuries inflicted may simply be that Elizabeth's killer was disturbed by the approached of Diemschutz with his pony and cart. It is now generally, although not universally, believed that the murderer, thwarted in the mutilation of his first victim, walked westwards into the City to find another. His return to Whitechapel, where he deposited the bloodstained fragment of Kate's apron, suggests that he was operating out of a base within the East End.

The name Jack the Ripper originated in a letter received by the Central News Agency on 27 September, little more than two days before the double murder. Neatly written in red ink, it purported to come from the murderer and promised further killings: 'I am down on whores and I shant quit ripping them till I do get buckled. Grand work the last job was. I gave the lady no time to squeal. How can they catch me now. I love my work and want to start again. You will soon hear of me with my funny little games . . . The next job I do I shall clip the lady's ears off and send to the police officers just for jolly wouldnt you.'

This macabre document was dated 25 September. It was addressed to 'The Boss, Central News Office' and was signed 'Jack the Ripper'.

Then, on 1 October, a day after the double killing, the Central News received another communication in the same handwriting. It was a postcard and it read: 'I wasnt codding dear old Boss when I gave you the tip. youll hear about saucy Jackys work tomorrow double event this time number one squealed a bit couldnt finish straight off. had not time to get ears for police.'

Both communications were forwarded to Scotland Yard. The police took them seriously enough to placard facsimiles outside police stations in the hope that someone would recognize the handwriting but there is nothing in the content of letter or postcard to suggest that they were actually written by the murderer. A more likely theory is that they were the work of a misguided journalist. This, indeed, became the police view. A suspicion developed at the Yard that Charles Moore and Tom Bulling of the Central News had concocted the hoax themselves but detectives were never able to procure conclusive evidence against them or anyone else.

Nevertheless, the practised penmanship of the Jack the Ripper letter, the absence of spelling mistakes, and the fact that it was sent to the Central News, which telegraphed news to the various papers and hence might afford it maximum publicity, all indicate a possible origin within journalism.

The Central News communications inspired a flood of similar letters. The grisliest was received by George Lusk, the chairman of the Mile End Vigilance Committee, on 16 October. It read: 'I send you half the Kidne I took from one women prasarved it for you tother piece I fried and ate it was very nise I may send you the bloody knif that took it out if you only wate a whil longer.' At the head of the letter were just two words: 'From hell'. With the letter was one half of a kidney. Dr Frederick Gordon Brown, the City Police surgeon, examined it to determine whether it could have been the kidney extracted from the body of Kate Eddowes. His report, apparently, was inconclusive. But he noted that the kidney was that of a human adult and that it had been preserved, not with formalin as it would have been had it come from a body delivered to a hospital for dissection, but in spirit.

Hundreds of similar letters still survive in the archives. But only in the case of the Lusk letter is there any evidence that the scribe may have been the murderer. These hoaxes wasted many hours of police time and helped sustain popular alarm.

MILLER'S COURT

The last murder generally attributed to Jack the Ripper occurred in the early hours of Friday 9 November 1888.

The victim was a young prostitute known to friends and neighbours as Mary Jane Kelly. She is the most mysterious of all the Ripper's victims.

Very little is known about her past. Joe Barnett, a market porter who lived with her

Body of Mary Kelly, as found in Miller's Court

for about 18 months, related what he knew of it at the inquest. By Barnett's account Mary was born in Limerick about 1863. The family emigrated to Wales when she was still a small child. John Kelly, Mary's father, found work as a foreman at an ironworks. Mary herself married a collier named Davies (or Davis) when she was about 16. The union was short-lived. After a few years Davies was killed in a mine explosion. Mary drifted. First to Cardiff, where she lived a 'bad life' with a cousin, and then, in 1884, to London. No verification for any of these statements has been discovered. However, the Cardiff censuses of 1871 and 1881 do record the family of an Irish immigrant named John Kelly living in Homfray Street. John had a daughter Mary, born in 1865 or 1867, and it is possible that she is the girl who became Jack the Ripper's last victim.

Miller's Court

Young and quite attractive, Mary found a succession of paramours in London. When not being supported by one of them she earned her living as a prostitute, first in a West End brothel, later on the streets of the East End. She met Joe Barnett in Commercial Street in 1887. The two decided to live together and at the beginning of 1888 they rented a tiny room, No. 13 Miller's Court, off Dorset Street in Spitalfields.

By the autumn of 1888 the couple were in serious difficulties. Barnett was unemployed, they had fallen behind with their rent and Mary had returned to prostitution. On 30 October, after a bitter quarrel, Barnett walked out. He was genuinely fond of Mary but he had always been unhappy about her trade. 'I have heard him say that he did not like her going out on the streets,' a neighbour remembered, 'He frequently gave her money, he was very kind to her, he said he would not live with her while she led that course of life.'

On the evening of 8 November Barnett visited Mary in Miller's Court, telling her that he was sorry he had no work and could not give her any money. It was the last time he saw her alive. After Barnett left that night Mary ventured into the streets in search of clients. Her rent was more than six weeks in arrears and she was desperately short of money.

At about 11.45 Mrs Mary Cox saw her returning to Miller's Court with a man. He was a shabbily dressed man in his mid-thirties, a man with a blotchy face and 'full carrotty moustache', carrying a quart can of beer.

About two hours later George Hutchinson, a

casual labourer, saw Mary pick up another client in Commercial Street. This man, dark and of Jewish appearance, sported a moustache curled up at the ends. He was very well dressed. Hutchinson remembered a dark felt hat, a long coat with collar and cuffs trimmed in astrakhan, and dark spats over button boots. A large gold watch-chain was displayed from his waistcoat and a horseshoe pin affixed in his tie. Hutchinson thought that he looked about 34 or 35 years old and stood about five feet six inches in height. He carried a small parcel in his left hand. Hutchinson followed the couple to Miller's Court and watched them go into No. 13. But although he waited outside until three o'clock he did not see them come out again.

At about four o'clock two of Mary's neighbours heard a scream of 'Murder!'

Neither took much notice because such cries were by no means unusual in the Victorian East End.

Later that morning, at about 10.45, John McCarthy, Mary's landlord, sent his assistant to No. 13 to collect rent. It was the day of the Lord Mayor's Show and McCarthy wanted to catch his tenant before she went out to see the procession. The assistant, Thomas Bowyer, was unable to get an answer at the door. Convinced that Mary was inside, however, he went round to a broken window, reached inside and pulled aside the curtain. Inside, heaped on a bedside table, were what appeared to be two lumps of flesh. Beyond, lying on the bed, was Mary's bloody and mutilated corpse.

A terrible sight awaited the police when they

burst into the room. Mary's body lay on its back, naked except for the remains of a linen undergarment. Dr Thomas Bond, one of the surgeons summoned to examine it, reported: 'The whole of the surface of the abdomen & thighs was removed & the abdominal cavity emptied of its viscera. The breasts were cut off, the arms mutilated by several jagged wounds & the face hacked beyond recognition of the features & the tissues of the neck were severed all round down to the bone.' The flesh from the abdomen and thighs were found on the bedside table. The viscera were found in various places around the body. The heart, extracted through the abdominal cavity, was missing and never recovered.

Extensive police inquiries throughout the district failed to unmask the murderer.

The house-to-house search in Whitechapel

After the double murder the Lord Mayor of London authorized a reward of £500 for information leading to the killer. The Metropolitan Police drafted extra men into the East End, made a house-to-house search of parts of Whitechapel and Spitalfields and experimented with bloodhounds. Adverse criticism by the press even stung a complacent Home Secretary into action and after the Miller's Court tragedy he authorized the police to offer a free pardon to any accomplice of the murderer who would betray him. All of these efforts proved futile.

It is not difficult to understand why the Ripper remained uncaught. In most murder cases the killer turns out to be a relative, friend or acquaintance of the victim. In the Whitechapel killings, however, careful investigations into the histories of the victims yielded no clue to the murderer, no motive for the crimes. And conventional methods of detection, resting heavily upon rewards and informers, were almost useless in the hunt for a lone killer.

In 1888 the major aids to detection were still years in the future. The first conviction of a criminal in Britain on the strength of fingerprints would not take place until 1902, the first to be secured by DNA patterns not until 1987. In the Ripper's day even the analysis of bloodstains was primitive. It was possible to determine whether blood was mammalian but not to prove that it was human or classify it by blood group.

After Miller's Court Jack the Ripper disappeared. There were a few Ripper-style slayings in the area after that date but these are generally regarded as copy murders.

Had the Ripper gone on killing he might have been caught red-handed. But in Victorian Whitechapel it is just as likely that he would have been able to carry on killing with impunity for years. The district was a bewildering maze of gloomy alleys, courts and backyards, impossibly large and complex for the police to patrol adequately. The victims, furthermore, themselves facilitated the murderer's efforts. As prostitutes, they were accustomed to accosting men in the streets and conducting them to dark, secluded byways and corners for sex.

The Ripper file at Scotland Yard was never closed. It is a case that remains unsolved.

WHO WAS
JACK THE RIPPER?

Although Jack the Ripper was never captured it is possible to deduce a little about him from the evidence of his crimes.

The statements of witnesses who gave descriptions of men seen with one or other of the victims suggest that the murderer was a white male of average or below average height in his twenties or thirties. Mrs Long, who saw a man talking with Annie Chapman just before the Hanbury Street murder, thought he was over forty but her evidence is compromised by the fact that she only saw the man's back. Most of the witnesses described men of 'shabby genteel' or 'respectable' appearance.

After the Mitre Square murder the killer is known to have escaped into Whitechapel. This, together with the close geographical grouping of all the crimes, indicates that he was probably a local man.

Five of the murders took place on weekends or public holidays. All six were committed between the hours of midnight and 6 a.m. It thus seems likely that the murderer was in some form of regular employment and that he was single, free to absent himself from home late at night.

Finally, the injuries inflicted by the Ripper provide clues. Most (though not all) of the doctors who examined Ripper victims concluded that the murderer possessed some degree of anatomical knowledge. Dr Brown, examining the body of Kate Eddowes, thought that he had displayed both anatomical knowledge and surgical skill in the extraction of the left kidney, a view that has been endorsed by modern medical opinion. The wounds also indicate that the Ripper was right-handed.

These factors must be borne in mind when suspects are assessed.

The police investigated hundreds of suspects during the hunt for Jack the Ripper. Only a few of the most important can be considered here.

Michael Ostrog

Michael Ostrog was a strange figure in the calendar of nineteenth-century criminals. His career of confidence trickery and theft spanned more than 40 years (1863–1904), punctuated by long terms of imprisonment.

In October 1888, after the double murder, the police tried to trace Ostrog in connection with the killings. It is not difficult to understand why. In March 1888, just five months before the murders began, he had been discharged from a lunatic asylum and it was believed that at some point in the more distant past he had once been a surgeon.

Sir Melville Macnaghten undoubtedly considered Ostrog an important suspect and listed him in 1894 as one of three men against

Dr Tumblety

whom the police held 'very reasonable suspicion'. According to Macnaghten, he was a 'homicidal maniac' whose whereabouts at the time of the murders could 'never be satisfactorily accounted for'.

Modern research has not upheld this assessment.

It now seems likely that Ostrog went to France after his discharge in March 1888. Certainly, on 14 November, five days after the Kelly murder, he was convicted of theft in Paris and sentenced to two years in prison.

Ostrog's height (five feet eleven inches) and age also tend to exonerate him. His exact date of birth is not known. But some sources make him nearly 60 in 1888 and by 1891, less than three years after the murders, his physical condition was described as 'much impaired' in hospital records.

Finally, Ostrog's criminal record refutes Macnaghten's contention that he was a homicidal maniac. Courteous, well-dressed and well-educated, his technique was to project a gentlemanly image in order to impose upon others and secure opportunities for petty theft. He never used violence against any of his victims. He was a suave deceiver, not a frenzied killer.

Dr Tumblety

A more plausible suspect was Dr Francis Tumblety.

Tumblety was a wealthy American quack doctor who made frequent visits to London. Reputedly homosexual, he was arrested in November 1888 and charged at Marlborough Street Police Court with 'unnatural offences'. He was then bailed to appear at the Central Criminal Court but immediately fled to France and from thence returned to America. He died in St Louis in 1903.

The police certainly regarded Tumblety as a serious Ripper suspect. As late as 1913 Ex-Chief Inspector John Littlechild, one-time head of the Special Branch, wrote of him as a 'very likely' suspect and told journalist George R. Sims that 'he was not known as a "Sadist" (which the murderer unquestionably was) but his feelings towards women were remarkable and bitter in the extreme.' It is also known that Tumblety owned a large collection of anatomical specimens. These included, by the report of one who saw them, about a dozen jars containing wombs from 'every class of women'.

If Tumblety was the Ripper his flight would explain why the murders suddenly ceased. But no reliable link between Tumblety and the East End has yet been established and in some ways the doctor does not match the existing evidence on the Ripper.

At 55 he was older than any of the men reportedly seen with victims. The murderer, furthermore, appears to have been a much smaller man. Annie Chapman and Kate Eddowes were both about five feet tall. Mrs Long thought that the man she saw with Annie stood only a 'little taller' than Annie, and Joseph Levy, one of the Jews thought to have seen Kate with a man near Mitre Square, said that the man was only 'about three inches taller than the woman'. Yet Tumblety was five feet ten inches or six feet in height. A lawyer who knew him said that he 'looked like a giant'.

Coroner Baxter's story of the American seeking specimens of the womb may refer to Tumblety but whether this incident had any bearing on the murders is difficult to say. The womb was removed from only two of the Ripper victims. In the case of Mary Kelly it was not, although the murderer clearly had the time to extract it had he so wished.

Ostrog and Tumblety were among the suspects investigated at the time of the murders. Fresh suspects continued to emerge in the years that followed.

Aaron Kosminski

In 1910 Sir Robert Anderson, head of CID at the time of the murders, published his memoirs. They contained some startling revelations.

By Anderson's account the Ripper was a low-class Polish Jew eventually 'caged in an asylum'. He was identified by the 'only person who had ever had a good view of the murderer' but the police were unable to charge him because the witness, who was also Jewish, refused to give evidence against a fellow Jew.

Although Anderson did not name the Polish Jew modern research has satisfactorily identified him as a poor immigrant barber named Aaron Kosminski. In 1888 Kosminski was 23 or 24 years old. He was committed to Colney Hatch Lunatic Asylum in 1891, and at that time Jacob Cohen, an acquaintance, alleged that he 'goes about the streets and picks up bits of bread out of the gutter & eats them, he drinks water from the tap & he refuses food at the hands of others. He took up a knife & threatened the life of his sister . . . He is melancholic, practises self-abuse. He is very dirty and will not be washed. He has not attempted any kind of work for years.' Kosminski was discharged from Colney Hatch to Leavesden Asylum near Watford in 1894 and died there in 1919.

Kosminski was identified by a witness. This

appears to have been the only time that the police procured tangible evidence to link a major suspect with the crimes. Unfortunately the identification was nothing like as conclusive as Anderson made it out to be.

The evidence available strongly suggests that the witness was Joseph Lawende, the commercial traveller believed to have seen the Ripper with Kate Eddowes on the night of the double murder. But this was a fleeting sighting, made in a dark street. And notes left by Chief Inspector Swanson prove that Kosminski cannot have been identified as the same man until 1890–91, two years or more after the event. At this distance from the original sighting identification evidence of this kind is practically worthless.

There are other difficulties in the case against Kosminski. He does not appear to have possessed any anatomical knowledge. Nor, despite Jacob Cohen, is there much evidence of a violent disposition. The doctors at Colney Hatch and Leavesden, who monitored his behaviour for more than 25 years, explicitly and repeatedly described him as a harmless patient.

Montague Druitt

SIr Melville Macnaghten held to a different theory.

Macnaghten joined the CID in 1889 and took charge of the department fourteen years later. He believed that the murders had prob-

ably been terminated by the killer's suicide
and his principal suspect was Montague John
Druitt, a schoolteacher and barrister who
threw himself into the Thames about three
weeks after the Miller's Court affair.

The reasons for Druitt's suicide are uncertain.
But it is known that he had just been fired
from his teaching post and that he left a note
for his brother. It read: 'Since Friday I felt I
was going to be like mother, and the best
thing for me was to die.' Ann Druitt, his
mother, had been committed to a lunatic
asylum in July 1888.

'From private information,' wrote
Macnaghten, 'I have little doubt but that his
own family believed him to have been the
murderer.' What the nature of this private
information was it is now impossible to

determine but it is unlikely to have been much more than hearsay. Certainly, if Druitt's relatives did suspect him they would not have told anyone else after his death because it would only have exposed them to distress and social embarrassment.

There are few other grounds for suspecting Druitt. As a surgeon's son he may have been competent to perform the mutilations. But there is no proof that he was a violent man and no evidence to connect him with the crimes or the East End.

Druitt's regular address was in Blackheath but he spent part of the late summer of 1888 on the south coast. A keen cricketer, he played several matches in Bournemouth in August and on 1 September, the day after Polly Nichols was murdered, was in Canford, Dorset, playing for the local team against

Wimborne. It is thus possible that Druitt was not even in London when the first two victims died.

George Chapman

The last major police suspect was George Chapman.

His real name was Severin Klosowski. Born in Poland, he came to London in 1887 as a young man of 21 and murdered three 'wives' by poison between 1897 and 1902. He was convicted of the third murder and executed in Wandsworth Prison in 1903.

There is no doubt that in 1903 Ex-Chief Inspector Abberline, the man who had coordinated the police hunt for the Ripper in Whitechapel, came to believe that Chapman and the Ripper were one and the same man. After the trial he congratulated Inspector Godley, who had arrested Chapman, with the words: 'You've got Jack the Ripper at last!' There is no doubt, too, that in many respects Chapman fits the Ripper evidence better than any other leading suspect.

Chapman was trained as a surgeon in Poland. He would thus have possessed sufficient medical expertise to commit the murders and would not have been squeamish about the use of the knife. His appearance matches descriptions of the Ripper exceedingly well. And in 1888 he was the proprietor of a barber's shop in Cable Street, within easy walking distance of all the murder sites. At that time, moreover, he was single and given

George Chapman

to staying out late at night. Above all, Chapman was sadistic and homicidal. Although he attracted a succession of female consorts he treated them all badly, threatening to behead one with a knife, menacing another with a revolver and physically beating several. Three were slowly tortured to death with poison.

It is important to remember, however, that no evidence linking Chapman to any of the Ripper crimes was ever procured. If Chapman was the Ripper, furthermore, we would have to accept that he abandoned the knife in favour of poison. Few criminologists have found such a dramatic change in *modus operandi* credible.

THE LEGEND

Within the CID there was never any consensus of opinion on the identity of Jack the Ripper. Different detectives espoused different theories. Some were honest enough to acknowledge publicly that the case had beaten them.

Today the mystery of Jack the Ripper continues to fascinate. Identity theories are published every year. All manner of celebrities are accused and in recent years the Duke of

Clarence (Queen Victoria's grandson), Sir William Gull (her Physician-in-Ordinary), Lord Randolph Churchill, Walter Sickert, Frank Miles and James Maybrick have all taken their turn in the dock. Such theories have nothing to do with history but they are testimony to the remarkable niche Jack the Ripper has carved for himself in popular culture.

The murders were so brutal and macabre that they attracted attention even in the dangerous East End of 1888. Interest was heightened by the press. Eager to exploit the spread of literacy spawned by Education Acts of 1870, 1876 and 1880, papers like the *Star* and the *Illustrated Police News* fuelled the excitement with lurid stories.

But there have been many notorious murder

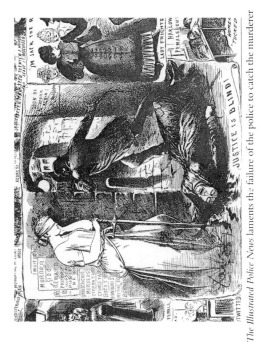

The Illustrated Police News laments the failure of the police to catch the murderer

cases since 1888, almost all of them forgotten, while the Ripper is still remembered. To some extent this is because he was the first sexual serial murderer of international repute. But mainly it is because he was never caught. It is the riddle of the killer's identity that, above all else, has kept his fame alive. The Ripper case is the classic 'whodunit'.

At its most innocuous 'Hunt the Ripper' is little more than an enjoyable parlour game. Yet there is a dark side to the legend. The events of 1888 were tragic. And they continue to inspire. 'I have read Jack the Ripper several times,' said Peter Kürten, the Düsseldorf killer of 1929–30. In Nottingham in 1978 a boy accused of murder told the court that his stepfather had urged him to stab the victim 'like Jack the Ripper'. Although such echoes of 1888 are thankfully rare they do occur.

Jack the Ripper played his part on the public stage for a mere three months. But for all that he has left us a potent and disturbing legacy.

FURTHER READING

There are numerous books about Jack the
Ripper, some good, the majority atrocious.
Alexander Kelly, *Jack the Ripper: A
Bibliography and Review of the Literature* (third
edition, Association of Assistant Librarians,
1995) is a safe guide through the minefield.

The standard general history of the murders is
Philip Sugden, *The Complete History of Jack the
Ripper* (Robinson, 1994). Stewart Evans and
Paul Gainey, *The Lodger: The Arrest & Escape*

of Jack the Ripper (Century, 1995) reveals important new evidence on Dr Tumblety. For concise information in quick-reference form, see Paul Begg, Martin Fido and Keith Skinner, *The Jack the Ripper A to Z* (revised edition, Headline, 1994).

A comprehensive book on the legend and mythology of Jack the Ripper is yet to be written. In the meantime Melvin Harris effectively demolishes some of the taller stories in *Jack the Ripper: The Bloody Truth* (Columbus, 1987) and *The True Face of Jack the Ripper* (Michael O'Mara, 1994).

Serious students of the case should subscribe to the specialists' quarterly, *Ripperana*, edited by Nick Warren and available from 16 Costons Avenue, Greenford, Middlesex, UB6 8RJ.

FURTHER MINI SERIES INCLUDE

HEROES OF THE WILD WEST

General Custer
Butch Cassidy and the Sundance Kid
Billy the Kid
Annie Oakley
Buffalo Bill
Geronimo
Wyatt Earp
Doc Holliday
Sitting Bull
Jesse James

FURTHER MINI SERIES INCLUDE

THEY DIED TOO YOUNG

Elvis
James Dean
Buddy Holly
Jimi Hendrix
Sid Vicious
Marc Bolan
Ayrton Senna
Marilyn Monroe
Jim Morrison

THEY DIED TOO YOUNG

Malcolm X
Kurt Cobain
River Phoenix
John Lennon
Glenn Miller
Isadora Duncan
Rudolph Valentino
Freddie Mercury
Bob Marley

FURTHER MINI SERIES INCLUDE

ILLUSTRATED POETS

Robert Burns
Shakespeare
Oscar Wilde
Emily Dickinson
Christina Rossetti
Shakespeare's Love Sonnets